CHECKERBOARD BIOGRAPHY LIBRARY

U.S. PRESIDENTS

The
United States Presidents

RUTHERFORD B. HAYES

ABDO Publishing Company

BreAnn Rumsch

visit us at
www.abdopublishing.com

Published by ABDO Publishing Company, 8000 West 78th Street, Edina, Minnesota 55439.
Copyright © 2009 by Abdo Consulting Group, Inc. International copyrights reserved in all
countries. No part of this book may be reproduced in any form without written permission from the
publisher. The Checkerboard Library™ is a trademark and logo of ABDO Publishing Company.

Printed in the United States.

Cover Photo: Corbis
Interior Photos: Alamy pp. 15, 19; Corbis p. 28; Getty Images p. 12; iStockphoto p. 32;
    Library of Congress pp. 5, 16, 17, 20, 22, 23, 25, 26; National Archives p. 14; North Wind p. 21;
    Public Domain pp. 27, 29; Rutherford B. Hayes Presidential Center pp. 9, 11

Editor: Heidi M.D. Elston
Art Direction & Cover Design: Neil Klinepier
Interior Design: Neil Klinepier

Library of Congress Cataloging-in-Publication Data

Rumsch, BreAnn, 1981-
  Rutherford B. Hayes / BreAnn Rumsch.
    p. cm. -- (The United States presidents)
  Includes bibliographical references and index.
  ISBN 978-1-60453-457-3
  1. Hayes, Rutherford Birchard, 1822-1893--Juvenile literature. 2. Presidents--United States--
Biography--Juvenile literature. I. Title.
  E682.R68 2009
  973.8'3092--dc22
  [B]
                        2008033925

CONTENTS

RUTHERFORD B. HAYES

Rutherford B. Hayes was the nineteenth president of the United States. He won one of the most contested presidential elections in U.S. history.

Hayes was born in Ohio. Growing up, he was a serious student. After college, Hayes became a successful lawyer. He won many of his cases.

During the American **Civil War**, Hayes joined the **Union** army. He fought bravely in numerous battles. Hayes was eventually promoted to **brevet** major general.

After the war, Hayes began his career in politics. He served in the U.S. House of Representatives. Later, he became governor of Ohio.

During his presidency, Hayes ended **Reconstruction**. He also worked for **civil service** reform. After leaving the White House, Hayes continued to work for reform. He devoted himself to helping others. Hayes was an honest leader who was dedicated to his country.

TIMELINE

1822 - On October 4, Rutherford Birchard Hayes was born in Delaware, Ohio.

1842 - Hayes graduated from Kenyon College in Gambier, Ohio.

1845 - Hayes graduated from Harvard Law School in Cambridge, Massachusetts.

1852 - On December 30, Hayes married Lucy Ware Webb.

1856 - Hayes helped establish Ohio's first Republican Party branch.

1858 - The city council of Cincinnati, Ohio, elected Hayes city solicitor.

1861 - On April 12, the American Civil War began; Hayes joined the Union army on June 7.

1864 - Hayes was elected to the U.S. House of Representatives, but did not take his seat.

1865 - The American Civil War ended on April 9; on June 8, Hayes resigned from the army; in December, he joined the House.

1867 - Hayes was elected governor of Ohio on October 8.

1869 - Hayes was reelected governor.

1875 - Hayes was elected to a third term as governor.

1877 - On March 2, Hayes was announced the winner of the presidential election; on March 3, he became the nineteenth U.S. president.

1878 - Hayes vetoed the Bland-Allison Act, but Congress passed it anyway.

1879 - The Specie Resumption Act went into effect on January 1.

1889 - Lucy Hayes died.

1893 - Rutherford B. Hayes died on January 17.

DID YOU KNOW?

Rutherford B. Hayes was the first president to take the oath of office at the White House. He was inaugurated there in the Red Room.

Hayes was the first president to put a telephone in the White House.

During Hayes's presidency, the Easter Egg Roll was held on the White House lawn for the first time in 1878. Children continue to enjoy this tradition today.

In 1880, Queen Victoria of the United Kingdom gave Hayes a desk. It was made from the timbers of the ship HMS *Resolute*. Almost every president since Hayes has used the *Resolute* desk.

Spiegel Grove, Hayes's home, is the site of the nation's first presidential library.

EARLY YEARS

Rutherford Birchard Hayes was born on October 4, 1822, in Delaware, Ohio. His nickname was Rud. Rud was the youngest of four children. He had one brother named Lorenzo and two sisters named Sarah and Fanny. Sadly, Lorenzo and Sarah died very young. Rud's father was also named Rutherford. He had died three months before Rud was born. Rud's mother was Sophia Birchard. Sophia was very protective of her two remaining children.

Growing up, Fanny and Rud stayed home with their mother. They did not go to school. The two became best friends. They ran in the fields, swam, fished, and told jokes. Rud and Fanny were happy. In 1836, Rud attended Norwalk Academy in Norwalk, Ohio. There, he studied speaking and writing. During the summer months, Rud studied Greek and Latin. In addition, Fanny taught him to speak French.

FAST FACTS

BORN - October 4, 1822

WIFE - Lucy Ware Webb (1831–1889)

CHILDREN - 8

POLITICAL PARTY - Republican

AGE AT INAUGURATION - 54

YEARS SERVED - 1877–1881

VICE PRESIDENT - William A. Wheeler

DIED - January 17, 1893, age 70

The next year, Rud attended Isaac Webb's **preparatory school** in Middletown, Connecticut. Rud was a good student. He studied many hours each day.

In 1838, Rud returned to Ohio. There, he attended Kenyon College in Gambier. Rud continued to study hard. He also did well in **debate**. In 1842, Rud graduated at the head of his class.

Rud (left) *with two of his classmates at Kenyon College*

LAW AND MARRIAGE

The following year, Hayes entered Harvard Law School in Cambridge, Massachusetts. He graduated in 1845. That same year, he passed his law examinations. Now Hayes could begin work as a lawyer.

Hayes opened his first law office in Lower Sandusky, Ohio. He practiced there for four years. Then in 1849, Hayes moved to Cincinnati, Ohio. There, he opened a law office.

Meanwhile, Hayes had met Lucy Ware Webb. They soon fell in love and were married on December 30, 1852. The Hayeses had eight children. Sadly, three died when they were young. Their surviving children were Birchard, Webb, Rutherford, Fanny, and Scott Russell.

Hayes's Cincinnati law firm was doing well. He successfully defended runaway slaves. Then in 1856, Hayes became involved in politics. He helped establish Ohio's first **Republican** Party branch.

In 1858, Cincinnati's city council elected Hayes city solicitor. As solicitor, he represented the city in court cases. He also advised city offices on the law. Hayes held this position until 1861.

The Hayeses on their
wedding day

CIVIL WAR SOLDIER

During this time, the North and the South were fighting over slavery. The North wanted to end slavery. The South thought each state should have slavery if it wanted to.

On April 12, 1861, the American **Civil War** began. Hayes joined the **Union** army on June 7. He was assigned to the Twenty-third Ohio Volunteer **Infantry** as a major.

Hayes fought battles in West Virginia and Virginia. He was soon promoted to lieutenant colonel. Later, he became colonel of the Seventy-ninth **Regiment**. On September 14, 1862, Hayes was wounded at the Battle of South Mountain. But he soon returned to the war.

In October 1864, **Republicans** from Cincinnati nominated Hayes for the U.S. House of Representatives. He accepted the nomination. But, he refused to leave his men in order to campaign. That year, Hayes was elected to the House. However, he was not ready to leave the army. The war was not yet over.

Hayes continued to fight for the army. He was wounded four more times. Then in December, he was promoted to brigadier general. On April 9, 1865, the **Confederates** surrendered. This ended the war. Hayes resigned on June 8. He left the army as a **brevet** major general.

Hayes liked being in the army. He was proud to fight for the freedom of all people.

RADICAL REPUBLICAN

In December 1865, Hayes joined the U.S. House of Representatives. In Congress, Hayes was a Radical **Republican**. Radical Republicans worked to protect the rights of freed slaves.

Hayes voted for the **Freedmen**'s Bureau Act. It gave food, medicine, and education to freed slaves in the South. It also helped them find work. In June 1866, Hayes voted for the Fourteenth **Amendment**. This amendment made all freedmen U.S. citizens.

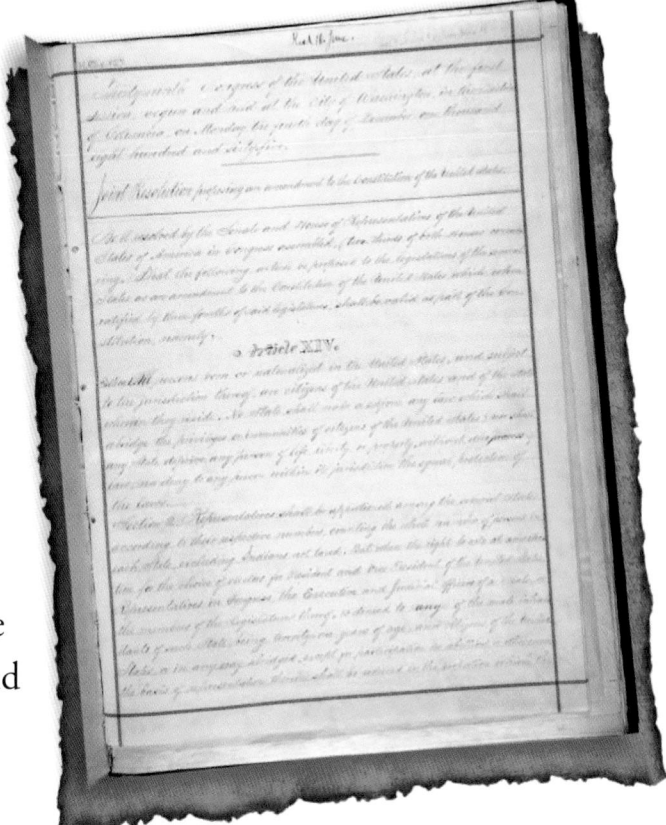

In 1868, the Fourteenth Amendment was approved by 28 of the 37 states. It became part of the U.S. Constitution on July 28.

Later that year, Hayes was reelected. In 1867, he voted for the **Reconstruction** Acts. According to the acts, Southern states had to elect new governments. They had to write new **constitutions** and promise voting rights to African-American men. Finally, they had to approve the Fourteenth **Amendment**.

Congressman Hayes served as chairman of the Joint Committee on the Library of Congress.

Many congressmen hoped the Tenure of Office Act would help Edwin M. Stanton keep his job.

Secretary of War Edwin M. Stanton was in charge of enforcing the **Reconstruction** Acts in the South. President Andrew Johnson did not approve of the acts. So, many congressmen worried Johnson would fire Stanton.

This led Hayes and other Radical **Republicans** to pass the Tenure of Office Act on March 2, 1867. This act said the president needed Senate approval to fire government officers.

President Johnson tried to fire Stanton anyway. Many congressmen thought Johnson should be **impeached**. Hayes agreed. In 1868, Congress voted to impeach President Johnson.

However, Hayes was not there to vote. He had resigned from the House of Representatives on August 7, 1867. Hayes had gone back to Ohio to campaign for governor.

Andrew Johnson was president from 1865 to 1869.

OHIO GOVERNOR

Back in Ohio, Hayes was elected governor on October 8, 1867. Governor Hayes worked for **civil service** reform. He did not believe in rewarding party members with government jobs. This is called the spoils system. Instead, he hired the people most qualified for each job.

Governor Hayes also worked for prison, welfare, and education reform. And, he oversaw the construction of a school for **deaf** children.

Meanwhile, Congress had proposed the Fifteenth **Amendment**. If passed, the amendment would guarantee **freedmen** the right to vote. Governor Hayes was in favor of the Fifteenth Amendment. It soon passed in Ohio. It was later added to the U.S. **Constitution**.

In 1869, Governor Hayes was reelected. During his second term, Hayes promoted **Republican** Ulysses S. Grant for president. He also supported building a state university.

Hayes helped establish the Agricultural and Mechanical College in Columbus, Ohio. It later became known as Ohio State University.

In addition, Governor Hayes wanted to study Ohio's mineral resources. He knew Ohio needed more mining and manufacturing businesses to remain successful. So in 1869, Hayes ordered a **geologic survey** of Ohio.

In 1872, Hayes retired from politics. He moved to Fremont, Ohio. There, the Hayes family settled in a home called Spiegel Grove. Soon, **Republicans** wanted Hayes to be governor again. In 1875, he was elected for a third term!

ELECTION OF 1876

A Republican campaign poster from 1876

Many **Republicans** believed Governor Hayes would be a strong presidential candidate. On June 14, 1876, Republicans nominated Hayes for president. They chose New York representative William A. Wheeler as his **running mate**.

The **Democratic** Party chose New York governor Samuel Tilden to run for president. Indiana governor Thomas A. Hendricks became his running mate.

The presidential election was held on November 7, 1876. Tilden received 184 electoral votes and Hayes received 165. To win, a candidate needed 185 electoral votes.

The election results in Louisiana, South Carolina, and Florida were contested. In those states, both the **Republican** and **Democratic** parties were claiming victory. So, 20 electoral votes remained unrewarded.

In January 1877, Congress established an Electoral Commission to settle the matter. The group included eight Republicans and seven Democrats. After much **debate**, the commission gave the contested electoral votes to Hayes. On March 2, 1877, Hayes was announced the winner!

Hayes was the only president whose election was decided by a congressional commission.

PRESIDENT HAYES

Hayes took office on March 3, 1877. In April, he withdrew the U.S. Army from Louisiana, South Carolina, and Florida. These states still had governments established by the **Reconstruction** Acts. The army enforced these governments. When the army withdrew, **Civil War** Reconstruction ended.

Next, Hayes wanted to make many **civil service** reforms. In June, he declared that federal civil servants should be forbidden from participating in politics. However, Congress disagreed.

Due to the disputed election results, Hayes was quietly inaugurated on March 3. His public inauguration took place on March 5.

SUPREME COURT APPOINTMENTS

JOHN MARSHALL HARLAN - 1877

WILLIAM B. WOODS - 1881

David M. Key

President Hayes and Congress also disagreed about the spoils system. Despite Congress's protests, he worked to end it. Hayes fired **Republicans** Chester Arthur and Alonzo B. Cornell from their jobs. He felt they had hired unqualified people.

And, many Republicans were upset when Hayes named David M. Key **postmaster general**. Key was a **Democrat**. He had also been an officer in the **Confederate** army during the **Civil War**. But, Hayes felt Key was the right man for the job.

Money was another important issue during Hayes's term. President Hayes supported the gold standard. This system allowed money to be exchanged for a fixed amount of gold.

Some people thought dollars should be made from silver as well as gold. So in 1878, Congress proposed the Bland-Allison Act. This act required the U.S. **Treasury** to buy $2 million in silver each month. The treasury also had to coin the silver into dollars.

Hayes knew that silver was worth less than gold. He felt it was unfair to receive silver dollars in exchange for gold dollars. So Hayes **vetoed** the act. However, Congress passed the act over his veto. The Bland-Allison Act became law that year.

In addition, much paper money had been issued during the **Civil War**. However, it was not backed by gold. So, Hayes ordered that the Specie Resumption Act be carried out. This act would allow people to trade their paper dollars for gold dollars. The Specie Resumption Act went into effect on January 1, 1879. As a result, the country's **economy** greatly improved.

President Hayes's Cabinet

March 3, 1877–March 4, 1881

- **STATE** – William M. Evarts
- **TREASURY** – John Sherman
- **WAR** – George W. McCrary
  Alexander Ramsey (from December 12, 1879)
- **NAVY** – Richard W. Thompson
  Nathan Goff Jr. (from January 6, 1881)
- **ATTORNEY GENERAL** – Charles Devens
- **INTERIOR** – Carl Schurz

Hayes with his cabinet

AFTER THE WHITE HOUSE

Hayes had accomplished much as president. However, he did not intend to run for a second term. In 1880, **Republican** James A. Garfield was elected president. In March 1881, Hayes and his family left the White House. They moved back to Spiegel Grove.

Back in Ohio, Hayes continued to work hard. He supported several colleges. These included Western Reserve University, Ohio Wesleyan University, and Ohio State University.

Hayes was also a **trustee** of the Peabody Educational Fund. This group worked to improve schools in the South. Later, Hayes became president of the

George Peabody, founder of the Peabody Educational Fund

Slater Fund. This organization raised money for the education of African Americans.

Education was not the only cause Hayes worked for. He also felt that reforming criminals would help prevent crime. So, he continued working to improve the prison system.

Spiegel Grove

Hayes also served as director of the First National Bank of Fremont. He often attended army reunions with other former **Civil War** soldiers. And he joined the New York **Civil Service** Reform Association.

Sadly, Lucy Hayes died in 1889. Hayes missed his wife deeply. But he kept busy with his work. He also enjoyed visiting with his family.

In January 1893, Hayes became ill while visiting friends in Cleveland, Ohio. He suffered from heart disease. On January 14, Hayes took a train back to Spiegel Grove. Rutherford B. Hayes died there on January 17, 1893.

Hayes enjoyed his wife's company. She was the first president's wife to have graduated from college.

Mr. and Mrs. Hayes are buried together at Spiegel Grove.

Rutherford B. Hayes was an important American leader. He fought bravely in the **Civil War**. He worked to secure rights for African Americans. He also supported public education and **civil service** reform. President Hayes only served one term. But, many of his ideas paved the way for future presidents.

OFFICE OF THE PRESIDENT

BRANCHES OF GOVERNMENT

The U.S. government is divided into three branches. They are the executive, legislative, and judicial branches. This division is called a separation of powers. Each branch has some power over the others. This is called a system of checks and balances.

EXECUTIVE BRANCH

The executive branch enforces laws. It is made up of the president, the vice president, and the president's cabinet. The president represents the United States around the world. He or she oversees relations with other countries and signs treaties. The president signs bills into law and appoints officials and federal judges. He or she also leads the military and manages government workers.

LEGISLATIVE BRANCH

The legislative branch makes laws, maintains the military, and regulates trade. It also has the power to declare war. This branch consists of the Senate and the House of Representatives. Together, these two houses make up Congress. Each state has two senators. A state's population determines the number of representatives it has.

JUDICIAL BRANCH

The judicial branch interprets laws. It consists of district courts, courts of appeals, and the Supreme Court. District courts try cases. If a person disagrees with a trial's outcome, he or she may appeal. If the courts of appeals support the ruling, a person may appeal to the Supreme Court. The Supreme Court also makes sure that laws follow the U.S. Constitution.

QUALIFICATIONS FOR OFFICE

To be president, a person must meet three requirements. A candidate must be at least 35 years old and a natural-born U.S. citizen. He or she must also have lived in the United States for at least 14 years.

ELECTORAL COLLEGE

The U.S. presidential election is an indirect election. Voters from each state choose electors to represent them in the Electoral College. The number of electors from each state is based on population. Each elector has one electoral vote. Electors are pledged to cast their vote for the candidate who receives the highest number of popular votes in their state. A candidate must receive the majority of Electoral College votes to win.

TERM OF OFFICE

Each president may be elected to two four-year terms. Sometimes, a president may only be elected once. This happens if he or she served more than two years of the previous president's term.

The presidential election is held on the Tuesday after the first Monday in November. The president is sworn in on January 20 of the following year. At that time, he or she takes the oath of office:

I do solemnly swear (or affirm) that I will faithfully execute the office of President of the United States, and will to the best of my ability, preserve, protect and defend the Constitution of the United States.

Line of Succession

The Presidential Succession Act of 1947 defines who becomes president if the president cannot serve. The vice president is first in the line of succession. Next are the Speaker of the House and the President Pro Tempore of the Senate. If none of these individuals is able to serve, the office falls to the president's cabinet members. They would take office in the order in which each department was created:

Secretary of State

Secretary of the Treasury

Secretary of Defense

Attorney General

Secretary of the Interior

Secretary of Agriculture

Secretary of Commerce

Secretary of Labor

Secretary of Health and Human Services

Secretary of Housing and Urban Development

Secretary of Transportation

Secretary of Energy

Secretary of Education

Secretary of Veterans Affairs

Secretary of Homeland Security

Benefits

• While in office, the president receives a salary of $400,000 each year. He or she lives in the White House and has 24-hour Secret Service protection.

• The president may travel on a Boeing 747 jet called Air Force One. The airplane can accommodate 70 passengers. It has kitchens, a dining room, sleeping areas, and a conference room. It also has fully equipped offices with the latest communications systems. Air Force One can fly halfway around the world before needing to refuel. It can even refuel in flight!

• If the president wishes to travel by car, he or she uses Cadillac One. Cadillac One is a Cadillac Deville. It has been modified with heavy armor and communications systems. The president takes Cadillac One along when visiting other countries if secure transportation will be needed.

• The president also travels on a helicopter called Marine One. Like the presidential car, Marine One accompanies the president when traveling abroad if necessary.

• Sometimes, the president needs to get away and relax with family and friends. Camp David is the official presidential retreat. It is located in the cool, wooded mountains in Maryland. The U.S. Navy maintains the retreat, and the U.S. Marine Corps keeps it secure. The camp offers swimming, tennis, golf, and hiking.

• When the president leaves office, he or she receives Secret Service protection for ten more years. He or she also receives a yearly pension of $191,300 and funding for office space, supplies, and staff.

PRESIDENTS AND THEIR TERMS

PRESIDENT	PARTY	TOOK OFFICE	LEFT OFFICE	TERMS SERVED	VICE PRESIDENT
George Washington	None	April 30, 1789	March 4, 1797	Two	John Adams
John Adams	Federalist	March 4, 1797	March 4, 1801	One	Thomas Jefferson
Thomas Jefferson	Democratic-Republican	March 4, 1801	March 4, 1809	Two	Aaron Burr, George Clinton
James Madison	Democratic-Republican	March 4, 1809	March 4, 1817	Two	George Clinton, Elbridge Gerry
James Monroe	Democratic-Republican	March 4, 1817	March 4, 1825	Two	Daniel D. Tompkins
John Quincy Adams	Democratic-Republican	March 4, 1825	March 4, 1829	One	John C. Calhoun
Andrew Jackson	Democrat	March 4, 1829	March 4, 1837	Two	John C. Calhoun, Martin Van Buren
Martin Van Buren	Democrat	March 4, 1837	March 4, 1841	One	Richard M. Johnson
William H. Harrison	Whig	March 4, 1841	April 4, 1841	Died During First Term	John Tyler
John Tyler	Whig	April 6, 1841	March 4, 1845	Completed Harrison's Term	Office Vacant
James K. Polk	Democrat	March 4, 1845	March 4, 1849	One	George M. Dallas
Zachary Taylor	Whig	March 5, 1849	July 9, 1850	Died During First Term	Millard Fillmore

PRESIDENT	PARTY	TOOK OFFICE	LEFT OFFICE	TERMS SERVED	VICE PRESIDENT
Millard Fillmore	Whig	July 10, 1850	March 4, 1853	Completed Taylor's Term	Office Vacant
Franklin Pierce	Democrat	March 4, 1853	March 4, 1857	One	William R.D. King
James Buchanan	Democrat	March 4, 1857	March 4, 1861	One	John C. Breckinridge
Abraham Lincoln	Republican	March 4, 1861	April 15, 1865	Served One Term, Died During Second Term	Hannibal Hamlin, Andrew Johnson
Andrew Johnson	Democrat	April 15, 1865	March 4, 1869	Completed Lincoln's Second Term	Office Vacant
Ulysses S. Grant	Republican	March 4, 1869	March 4, 1877	Two	Schuyler Colfax, Henry Wilson
Rutherford B. Hayes	Republican	March 3, 1877	March 4, 1881	One	William A. Wheeler
James A. Garfield	Republican	March 4, 1881	September 19, 1881	Died During First Term	Chester Arthur
Chester Arthur	Republican	September 20, 1881	March 4, 1885	Completed Garfield's Term	Office Vacant
Grover Cleveland	Democrat	March 4, 1885	March 4, 1889	One	Thomas A. Hendricks
Benjamin Harrison	Republican	March 4, 1889	March 4, 1893	One	Levi P. Morton
Grover Cleveland	Democrat	March 4, 1893	March 4, 1897	One	Adlai E. Stevenson
William McKinley	Republican	March 4, 1897	September 14, 1901	Served One Term, Died During Second Term	Garret A. Hobart, Theodore Roosevelt

PRESIDENT	PARTY	TOOK OFFICE	LEFT OFFICE	TERMS SERVED	VICE PRESIDENT
Theodore Roosevelt	Republican	September 14, 1901	March 4, 1909	Completed McKinley's Second Term, Served One Term	Office Vacant, Charles Fairbanks
William Taft	Republican	March 4, 1909	March 4, 1913	One	James S. Sherman
Woodrow Wilson	Democrat	March 4, 1913	March 4, 1921	Two	Thomas R. Marshall
Warren G. Harding	Republican	March 4, 1921	August 2, 1923	Died During First Term	Calvin Coolidge
Calvin Coolidge	Republican	August 3, 1923	March 4, 1929	Completed Harding's Term, Served One Term	Office Vacant, Charles Dawes
Herbert Hoover	Republican	March 4, 1929	March 4, 1933	One	Charles Curtis
Franklin D. Roosevelt	Democrat	March 4, 1933	April 12, 1945	Served Three Terms, Died During Fourth Term	John Nance Garner, Henry A. Wallace, Harry S. Truman
Harry S. Truman	Democrat	April 12, 1945	January 20, 1953	Completed Roosevelt's Fourth Term, Served One Term	Office Vacant, Alben Barkley
Dwight D. Eisenhower	Republican	January 20, 1953	January 20, 1961	Two	Richard Nixon
John F. Kennedy	Democrat	January 20, 1961	November 22, 1963	Died During First Term	Lyndon B. Johnson
Lyndon B. Johnson	Democrat	November 22, 1963	January 20, 1969	Completed Kennedy's Term, Served One Term	Office Vacant, Hubert H. Humphrey
Richard Nixon	Republican	January 20, 1969	August 9, 1974	Completed First Term, Resigned During Second Term	Spiro T. Agnew, Gerald Ford

PRESIDENT	PARTY	TOOK OFFICE	LEFT OFFICE	TERMS SERVED	VICE PRESIDENT
Gerald Ford	Republican	August 9, 1974	January 20, 1977	Completed Nixon's Second Term	Nelson A. Rockefeller
Jimmy Carter	Democrat	January 20, 1977	January 20, 1981	One	Walter Mondale
Ronald Reagan	Republican	January 20, 1981	January 20, 1989	Two	George H.W. Bush
George H.W. Bush	Republican	January 20, 1989	January 20, 1993	One	Dan Quayle
Bill Clinton	Democrat	January 20, 1993	January 20, 2001	Two	Al Gore
George W. Bush	Republican	January 20, 2001	January 20, 2009	Two	Dick Cheney
Barack Obama	Democrat	January 20, 2009			Joe Biden

"He serves his party best who serves his country best."

Rutherford B. Hayes

WRITE TO THE PRESIDENT

You may write to the president at:

The White House
1600 Pennsylvania Avenue NW
Washington, DC 20500

You may e-mail the president at:
comments@whitehouse.gov

GLOSSARY

amendment - a change to a country's constitution.

brevet - a military title given to an officer who has a higher rank than he or she is paid for.

civil service - the part of the government that is responsible for matters not covered by the military, the courts, or the law. A civil servant is someone who works for this part of the government.

civil war - a war between groups in the same country. The United States of America and the Confederate States of America fought a civil war from 1861 to 1865.

Confederate - relating to the Confederate States of America. This country was formed by the states of South Carolina, Georgia, Florida, Alabama, Louisiana, Mississippi, Texas, Virginia, Tennessee, Arkansas, and North Carolina when they left the Union between 1860 and 1861.

constitution - the laws that govern a country or a state. The U.S. Constitution is the laws that govern the United States.

deaf - wholly or partly unable to hear.

debate - a contest in which two sides argue for or against something.

Democrat - a member of the Democratic political party. When Rutherford B. Hayes was president, Democrats supported farmers and landowners.

economy - the way a nation uses its money, goods, and natural resources.

freedman - a person freed from slavery.

geologic survey - the mapping of an area of land relating to its structure and composition, including its natural resources.

impeach - to charge a public official with misconduct in office.

infantry - soldiers trained and organized to fight on foot.

postmaster general - an official in charge of the U.S. Postal Service.

preparatory school - a typically private school that prepares students for college.

Reconstruction - the period after the American Civil War when laws were passed to help the Southern states rebuild and return to the Union.

regiment - a large military unit made up of troops.

Republican - a member of the Republican political party. When Rutherford B. Hayes was president, Republicans supported business and strong government.

running mate - a candidate running for a lower-rank position on an election ticket, especially the candidate for vice president.

secretary of war - a member of the president's cabinet who handles the nation's defense.

treasury - a place where money is kept.

trustee - a person in charge of another person's or an organization's property or affairs.

Union - relating to the states that remained in the United States during the American Civil War.

veto - the right of one member of a decision-making group to stop an action by the group. In the U.S. government, the president can veto bills passed by Congress. But Congress can override the president's veto if two-thirds of its members vote to do so.

WEB SITES

To learn more about Rutherford B. Hayes, visit ABDO Publishing Company on the World Wide Web at **www.abdopublishing.com**. Web sites about Rutherford B. Hayes are featured on our Book Links page. These links are routinely monitored and updated to provide the most current information available.

INDEX